INSTANT POT DUO PLUS Cookbook

100 Easy & Delicious Recipes

For Your Instant Pot Duo Plus and Other Instant Pot Electric Pressure Cookers (Vegan Recipes Included)

By
JERRY POTMAN

ISBN: 978-1-950284-35-1

Disclaimer

Please note, the information contained in this book, are for educational purposes only. Every attempt has been made to provide accurate, up to date and reliable complete information. By reading this document, the reader agrees that under no circumstances are we responsible for any losses, direct or indirect, which are incurred as a result of the use of the information contained in this document, including but not limited to errors, omissions or inaccuracies.

Table of Contents

INTRODUCTION

Hello and welcome to this book: Instant Pot DUO PLUS Cookbook containing over 100 unique Easy & Delicious Recipes For Your Instant Pot Duo Plus and Other Instant Pot Electric Pressure Cookers.

The book being the first cookbook for the new wonder kid (IP Duo Plus) is written and well formatted with the beginners at heart to make for easy understanding. It will help get you from beginner to pro in no time, and see to it that you make and enjoy healthy homemade meals with your new instant pot.

I hope you enjoy this book as I did writing it.

CHAPTER 1: ABOUT INSTANT POT DUO PLUS

Instant Pot Duo Plus, the successor of the bestselling instant pot duo, is the next evolution in the Duo Series, and currently the No. 1 best-selling cooker in the Instant Pot family.

The cooker is a 9-in-1 Programmable kitchen appliance with advanced microprocessor technology which incorporates in it all of the great features that made the Duo a household name. It has new and improved programs and features to continually support one's fast-paced, health-conscious and lifestyle.

It has on it, 3 new preset buttons namely - **Cake**, **Egg**, and **Sterilize**. And also includes the yogurt function found on other IP duo series, but not some of the other makes.

With the IP duo Plus, you will enjoy a whole new

- Large LCD Screen with Digital Display
- Mute button for those beeps in the night when cooking.
- Plus +/ -Minus button for both time and pressure
- Keep Warm Selector can be selected to ON or OFF at any time.
- Delay start of 24 hours and keep warm for 10 hours.
- Lid rest (right or left side)

INSTANT POT BENEFITS

On a norm, pressure cookers are a proficient, versatile, safe, and easy to use. They make better tasting and, healthier food that is cooked in less time and with less energy.

Without any doubt, it is now clear that many households are gradually shifting toward this approach. As the use of pressure cooking has increased ever since people found out how safe, comforting and easy it is to prepare meals that are not just healthy but delicious as well with an electric pressure cooker.

The instant pot which happens to be the most sort out electric pressure cooker is not left out of the goodies too. With it, you will notice;

- Your food cooking time is reduced by 80 to 90 percent
- Nutrient retention increases to as high as 90 percent
- Makes way for better digestibility
- Fewer cooking side effects

That said, the added advantage of preparing bone broth in the instant pot is the tremendous health benefits of broth. Research has shown that rich marrow present in the bones which serve as the number 1 essential for cellular health i.e. red blood cells, transport oxygen etc are better extracted and retained when pressure cooked.

INSTANT POT DUO PLUS PRESSURE COOKING TIPS

Today, instant pot pressure cookers are termed wonder cookers. They're like small time machines that propel you into the future. Where you don't have to worry about what's for dinner!

Cooking time is halved. Leaving you with more than enough time to focus on other things. It's dammed easy to use with lots of awesome food list. However, to get the best out of your instant pot, here come a few tips to follow.

1. For better flavors, you might want to first, sauté the aromatic vegetables like onions, celery, and bell peppers in a little oil/fat in your instant pot before proceeding with other ingredients. Mind you, this is usually done with the sauté function while the lid is off.

2. Meats require browning. So, consider browning them in a little oil using the saute function before adding additional ingredients. Be sure not to do this with the lid on.

3. To avoid having less than enough water required for pressure buildup or cooking the food, it's usually better to allow the cooker cool after browning before adding water. This is simply because adding water while the cooker is still hot might lead to evaporation and reduction in the amount of liquid needed for the food.

4. Thin down thick sauces with small water so they don't cake up and burn to the bottom of the pot. This can make pressure buildup to fail.

5. Thicken sauces after the food is completely cooked in your instant pot using the sauté function and simmering until the desired consistency is reached.

6. Ingredients like vegetables that cook faster than others should be added at the end of cooking. To do this, simply make use of quick release and add the supposed ingredient.

7. Be sure to always follow the pressure release method given in the recipe. As this can contribute a lot to the taste and degree of doneness.

SAFETY PRESSURE COOKING TIPS

Overfilling the Instant Pot

The mistake most new users make is filling their Instant Pot with food & liquid up to the Max Line. This will no doubt lead to clogging of the Venting Knob.

Using Quick Release For Foamy Food or When Cooker is Overfilled

Foamy recipes like applesauce should never undergo quick release. As the result is rather messy.

Many pressure cooker new users are unsure when to use the Quick and Natural Pressure Release. For foamy foods like grains and beans, the chances of getting your food splatter through the vent knob are high.

The best remedy to this, is to simply make use of Natural Release for foamy food or when the pot is overfilled. But if the recipe calls for quick release, then do it gradually. You don't have to turn the Venting Knob all the way to Venting Position to release pressure.

Cooking Liquid: Too Thick/Not Enough Liquid

Another mistake many do is not adding enough water before sealing the lid for pressure cooking. And ideally, if there is not enough cooking liquid or the liquid in it is too thick, your Instant Pot will not be able to build up enough steam to reach pressure.

To avoid making such mistake, we recommend using a minimum of 1 cup of liquid for every meal until you get comfortable with the machine. And be sure to always add thickeners such as flour, cornstarch, or arrowroot after the pressure cooking cycle.

Safest Way to Open the Lid

From experience, the safest way to open your cooker lid is by slowly tilting it away from you. This can be done with the help of a spoon, wood or any long object to avoid burns from the steam.

CHAPTER 2: BREAKFAST

Braised Cabbage

Chopping and preparing the vegetables is the most time-consuming part of this easy recipe, which cooks equally fast on the instant pot as it does on conventional cookers.

Serves 4

Ingredients

1 tbsp sesame seed oil

1 medium cabbage (about 3 pounds) (divided into 8 wedges)

1 medium carrot, grated (about ¾ cup)

1 ¼ cups + 2 tsp water (divided)

¼ cup apple cider vinegar

1 tsp raw demerara sugar

½ tsp cayenne powder

½ tsp red pepper flakes

2 tsp cornstarch

How You Make It:

1. Preheat the instant pot duo plus using the saute function.

2. Add the oil and brown the cabbage wedges in it on one side (takes 3 mins).

3. Add the 1 ¼ cups of water, sugar, vinegar, cayenne, and hot pepper flakes. Swish around and include the cabbage wedges.

4. Brown with side facing up and sprinkle the carrots on top.

5. Close the lid. Select pressure and pressure cook at high for 5 mins.

6. When done, release pressure using the quick method. Arrange the wedges and any loose leaves in a dish.

7. Bring the cooking liquid to a boil using the saute function. Mix the cornstarch with the 2 tsp of water and pour into pot.

8. Allow to simmer until thickened. Pour over the cabbage wedges and serve.

Morning Oatmeal

Prep Time: 5 mins

Cook Time: 30 mins

Total Time: 35 mins

Servings: 4

Ingredients

2 gala apples (peeled or unpeeled but roughly sliced)

1 cup (160g) regular steel cut oats

2 ½ cups cold water

1 tsp (5ml) vanilla extract

A pinch of salt

1 tbsp unsalted butter

1 cinnamon stick

½ tsp ground nutmeg

½ tsp allspice, grounded

½ tsp fresh ginger, grated

Sweetener

Honey, Maple syrup, or Brown sugar

Garnish

1 gala apple, sliced

How You Make It:

1. Preheat your instant pot duos or any other model using the saute button.

2. Melt 1 tbsp unsalted butter in it and toast 1 cup steel cut oats until fragrant (takes 2 mins).

3. When done, add 2 roughly sliced gala apples, vanilla extract, cinnamon stick, ½ tsp nutmeg, ½ tsp allspice, grated fresh ginger, and a pinch of salt.

4. Mix and pour in 2 ½ cups of cold water to submerge the steel cut oats.

5. Close the lid, pressure cook at High for 10 mins and use natural Release method.

6. Stir with a silicone spatula to break up the apple slices and thicken the oatmeal.

7. Sweeten with either honey, maple syrup or brown sugar.

8. Serve garnished with thinly sliced apple.

Hard Boiled Eggs

Prep: 1 min
Cook: 14 mins
Total: 15 mins
Serving: 6 - 8 eggs

Ingredients

6 - 8 large eggs straight from the fridge
1 cup (250ml) cold water

How You Make It:

1. Insert a trivet into your IP. Pour 1 cup of water in and place the eggs on the trivet.

2. Close the lid. Push the pressure button, adjust to either High Pressure for 8 mins + Quick Release or Low Pressure for 12 mins + Quick Release

3. When done, open the lid.

4. Carefully peel the eggs under cold running water and serve immediately.

Note: If not serving immediately, be sure to stop the cooking process by submerging the eggs in a bowl of cold water for roughly 5 mins.

Deviled Eggs

Prep: 5 mins
Cook: 25 mins
Total: 30 mins
Serving: 12 - 16 deviled eggs

Ingredients

6 - 8 large eggs
1 cup (250ml) cold water
Paprika

Dressing:

2 tbsp full-fat mayonnaise
1 tbsp extra-virgin olive oil
1 tsp dijon mustard
1 tsp white vinegar
¼ - ½ tsp sriracha
Ground black pepper and sea salt to taste

How You Make It:

1. Insert the steamer basket into the instant pot. Pour in 1 cup of cold water and place 6 - 8 large eggs onto the steamer basket.

2. Close the lid, select pressure and cook at Low Pressure for 12 mins + Quick Release when done.

3. Carefully open the lid, take out the eggs and peel under cold running water.

4. If not ready to peel, stop the cooking process by submerging the eggs in a cold water for roughly 5 mins.

5. After peeling, slice in half. Carefully remove the yolks and mash in a small mixing bowl with a fork. (set aside the egg whites).

6. For the dressing, Add all the ingredients to the mashed egg yolks. Mix well.

7. Pipe the Dressing by placing the dressing mixture in a small Ziploc bag. With a pair of scissors, cut a small corner. Then, pipe the dressing mixture into the egg whites.

8. Serve garnished with paprika.

Tomato Quiche

Yield: 6 servings

Print Recipe

Ingredients:

12 large eggs

½ tsp salt

¼ tsp fresh ground black pepper

1 cup diced seeded tomato

½ cup milk

3 cups fresh baby spinach (roughly chopped)

3 large green onions (sliced)

 4 tomato slices for topping the quiche

¼ cup shredded Parmesan cheese

How You Make It:

1. First, put a trivet in the IP bottom and add 1 ½ cups water.

2. Next, whisk together the eggs, milk, salt and pepper in a bowl.

3. In a 1 ½ quart baking dish, add the spinach, tomato, and green onions: mix well.

4. Now, pour the egg mixture over veggies and stir to combine.

5. Place the sliced tomatoes over then and sprinkle with Parmesan cheese.

6. With the help of a sling, gently lower the dish on the trivet inside the IP duo plus or any instant pot pressure cooker (This should help when bringing it out).

7. Lock the lid in place. Select High Pressure with 20 mins cook time (10 mins natural + quick pressure release when done).

8. Open the lid, lift out the dish and broil until lightly browned if desired.

Chinese Congee Recipe

Prep: 5 mins

Cook: 60 mins

Total: 1 hr 5 mins

Serving: 2 - 4

Ingredients

⅔ pound ground beef

65 grams spinach (chopped)

¾ cup Jasmine rice

7 cups cold water

1 stalk green onion (chopped)

Ground Beef Marinade

⅓ tsp fine sea salt

¼ tsp sesame oil

⅓ tsp ground white pepper

How You Make It:

1. First, marinate ⅔ lb ground beef with ¼ tsp sesame oil, ⅓ tsp fine sea salt, and ⅓ tsp white pepper for 20 mins in a mixing bowl.

2. When done, add ¾ cup of rice, marinated ground beef, and 7 cups of water to the IP duo plus.

3. Close the lid and cook at High for 25 mins (Use natural release for 18 mins).

4. Open the lid and thicken the Congee using the saute function.

5. Add the chopped spinach and continue heating with the saute function.

6. At this point, stir until desired thickness & consistency is reached.

7. Season with salt and serve garnished with green onions

8. Could be served alongside your favorite main dishes.

Farro

Yield: 4 servings

Ingredients:

2 tbsp butter

2 cups water

¼ cup raisins

1 (8.8 oz.) package Trader Joe's pre-cooked Farro

¼ cup packed brown sugar

½ tsp vanilla extract

¼ tsp cinnamon

¼ tsp salt

How You Make It:

1. Push sauté on your IP DUO Plus or any other model, and melt the butter in it.

2. Once melted, stir in farro and cook, stirring frequently, until fragrant (takes 3 mins).

3. Add water, brown sugar, vanilla, raisins, cinnamon, and salt.

4. Close the lid, and cook at High Pressure for 5 mins (5 mins naturally release + quick release).

5. Open the cooker, stir the mixture.

6. You can serve topped with additional brown sugar and a splash of milk.

French Toast

Yield: 6-8 servings

Ingredients:

Cranberry Orange Sauce

2 cups fresh cranberries (washed)

½ cup granulated sugar

¼ tsp salt

¼ cup fresh orange juice

¼ tsp ground cinnamon

French Toast

4 tbsp butter (melted)

2 cups whole milk

½ cup sugar

Finely grated zest from 1 orange

¼ tsp salt

3 eggs (beaten)

1 tsp vanilla extract

1 loaf Challah bread (cubed)

How You Make It:

1. Add the first set of ingredients to a saucepan and bring to a boil over medium heat.

2. Continue cooking until the berries have popped and slightly thickened (5 mins).

3. When done, pour into a buttered 7×3" cake pan, glass or baking dish that fits perfectly in your IP.

4. Whisk together, the melted butter and ½ cup sugar in a bowl. Add milk, orange zest, vanilla, beaten eggs, and salt.

5. Next, mix in cubed bread and let rest until the bread absorbs the milk.

6. Stir and spread bread mixture on top of cranberry sauce in pan.

7. After that, prepare a foil sling for easy lifting of the dish by taking an 18" strip of foil, and folding lengthwise twice.

8. At this point, pour 1 cup of water into your instant pot and insert the trivet.

9. Center the pan on the foil strip from step 7, and lower it into the cooker.

10. Seal the lid. Select High Pressure with 25 mins cook time (Quick Release).

11. Carefully open the lid once the pressure drops and remove the dish.

12. You can serve immediately, or broil to brown the top.

CHAPTER 3: STOCKS & BROTH WITH IP DUO PLUS

Homemade Chicken Stock

Ingredients:

1 (4 lb) whole chicken

2 large carrots (chopped)

3 smashed garlic cloves

1 large onion (chopped)

2 celery stalks, chopped

5 sprigs fresh parsley

1 bay leaf

3 sprigs fresh thyme

½ Tsp whole peppercorns

8 cups of water

How You Make It:

1. Simply add all the ingredients to your IP duo plus or any instant pot model and secure the lid.

2. Press the Pressure cook button, and adjust the time to 20 mins then allow to begin pressure cooking (Use 15 mins natural release)

3. Open the lid and allow the stock to cool a bit.

4. Pour through a fine mesh strainer, then refrigerate covered

5. You can skim the fats once chilled.

Beef Bone Broth

Preparation time: 5 mins

Cooking time: 1 hour, 30 mins

Total time: 2 hours, 30 mins

Makes 8 cups

Ingredients:

2 ½ pounds beef bones (that is: short ribs, knuckles, oxtails, and more)

1 yellow onion (quartered)

1 carrot (cut into large chunks)

1 tsp extra-virgin olive oil

2 celery stalks (quartered)

1 tbsp fish sauce (optional)

1 bay leaf 2 tsp apple cider vinegar

8 cups water

How You Make It:

1. Begin by preheating the oven to 400 ° F.

2. After that, toss the bones with the oil on a baking sheet.

3. Roast in the oven for 30 mins and allow to cool

4. Add the bones, alongside the rest ingredients to your instant pot and secure the lid.

5. Select pressure cook and cook for 1 ½ hours at high pressure. (use 15 mins natural release + quick release).

6. Open and allow to cool, after which you skim any fat off the top of the stock.

7. Now, carefully strain the broth using a fine mesh strainer.

8. You can store in the refrigerator for a few days or up to 3 months in the freezer.

Spicy Chicken Bone Broth

Prep time: 5 mins

Total time: 2 hours 10 mins

Makes 8 cups

Ingredients:

2 ½ pounds mixed chicken bones and feet

1 celery stalk (quartered)

1 (1 ½-inch) piece ginger (peeled & cut into ¼-inch slices)

1 tsp whole black peppercorns

1 yellow onion (quartered)

1 carrot, cut into large chunks

1 tbsp fish sauce

1 tsp apple cider vinegar

8 cups water

How You Make It:

1. Simply add all the ingredients to your IP and secure the lid.

2. Select pressure cook and cook for 1 ½ hours at high pressure. (use 15 mins natural release + quick release).

3. Open the lid and skim any fat off the top of the stock.

4. Strain the broth with the help of a fine-mesh strainer.

5. Store in the refrigerator for a few days or freeze for 2 to 3 months.

Fish Broth

Ingredients:

3 pounds thoroughly rinsed fish heads and bones

1 large onion, quartered (no need to peel)

1 rib celery (cut into chunks)

6 cups water (plus more as needed)

A few leek greens (optional)

2 large bay leaves

¼ tsp whole black peppercorns

How You Make It:

1. Simply add all the ingredients to your IP and secure the lid.

2. Select pressure cook and cook for 8 mins at high pressure. (use 15 mins natural release + quick release).

3. When done, strain into one or more storage containers.

4. You can press the solids to release all the liquid into the containers after which you then discard.

5. Chill and remove congealed fat.

6. You can boil the broth vigorously until reduced for a more concentrated flavor.

7. Refrigerate for up to 4 days or freeze for 2 to 3 months.

Shrimp Broth

Makes 2 to 3 cups

Ingredients:

peelings from 1 pound shrimp (about 2 ½ cups)

1 large onion, quartered (no need to peel)

1 carrot (cut into chunks)

2 large bay leaves

enough water to cover

A few leek greens (optional)

1 rib celery (cut into chunks)

¼ tsp whole black peppercorns

How You Make It:

1. Throw all the ingredients into your IP duos or any instant pot model and secure the lid.

2. Select pressure cook and cook for 5 mins at high pressure. (use 15 mins natural release + quick release).

3. Carefully open the lid and strain into one or more storage containers.

4. You can press the solids to release all the liquid into the containers after which you then discard.

5. Chill and remove congealed fat.

6. You can boil the broth vigorously until reduced for a more concentrated flavor.

7. Refrigerate for up to 4 days or freeze for 2 to 3 months.

CHAPTER 4: SOUPS, STEWS & SAUCES

Ethiopian-Style Spinach & Lentil Soup

Serves 4 to 6

Ingredients

2 tbsp unsalted butter

1 medium red onion (chopped)

2 tsp ground coriander

½ tsp cinnamon powder

¼ tsp clove powder

1 tbsp olive oil

1 tsp garlic powder

½ tsp turmeric powder

¼ tsp cardamom powder

8 cups water

¼ tsp pepper

¼ tsp cayenne pepper

¼ tsp fresh grated nutmeg

2 cup brown lentils

2 tsp salt

6 oz. fresh spinach or baby spinach (about 4 packed cups)

4 tbsp lemon juice

How You Make It:

1. Preheat your IP using the sauté function.

2. After that, you add the butter, oil, garlic, coriander, onion, cinnamon, turmeric, cayenne, cardamom, clove, and nutmeg.

3. Sauté this for three mins and include the lentils and water.

4. Secure the lid. Select pressure cook and cook for 10 mins at high pressure. (use natural release).

5. Carefully open the lid. Add salt and pepper to pot and mix in the spinach leaves.

6. Finally, stir in the fresh lemon juice and serve.

Best Ham and Bean Soup

Prep time: 20 mins

Cook time: 1 h 10 m

Total time: 2 hours 50 mins

12 servings

154 cal

Ingredients

1 cup dry navy beans

3 cups water (+3 cups water)

6 tbsp chopped fresh parsley

1 large meaty smoked ham bone

2 whole bay leaves

3 tbsp dried minced onion flakes

½ tsp dried thyme leaves

1 tbsp minced fresh garlic

½ tsp dry mustard powder

½ tsp chili powder

5 cups water

1 tbsp olive oil

½ tsp paprika

1 cup sliced celery

1 (28 oz.) can tomato puree

½ cup ketchup

3 tbsp chicken soup base

3 tbsp molasses

1 tbsp brown sugar

¼ tsp cracked black pepper, or to taste

½ cup uncooked small shell pasta

How You Make It:

1. First, bring the dry beans and 3 cups of water to a boil in a saucepan.

2. Once achieved, remove from heat, and allow to cool for 1 hour then, drain and rinse.

3. Pour the extra 3 cups of water in your instant pot and add the soaked beans along with the ham bone, parsley, bay leaves, dried onion flakes, thyme, dry mustard, garlic, chili powder, and paprika.

4. Secure the lid. Select pressure cook and cook for 10 mins at high pressure. (use natural release).

5. Open the lid and pour in additional 5 cups of water.

6. Add celery, olive oil, chicken soup base, ketchup, molasses, tomato puree, brown sugar, and cracked black pepper.

7. After that, bring to a boil, using the saute function at "more". Once that is achieved, reduce to less and simmer the soup until the beans are tender (take 45 mins).

8. At this point, stir in the shell pasta. Simmer until the pasta is tender.

Irish Beef Stew

Prep: 10 mins

Cook: 100 mins

Total: 1 hr 50 mins

Serving: 4 - 6

Ingredients

2 pounds chuck steak (1.5 inch in thickness)

8 cremini mushrooms (quartered)

1 large onion (sliced)

4 medium garlic cloves (minced)

1 medium shallot (minced) (Optional)

2 medium carrots (cut into chunks)

1 large russet potatoes (cut into 8 pieces)

2 sprigs thyme

1 sprig rosemary

1 bay leaf

12 grams 70% dark chocolate

2 tbsp olive oil

1 ½ tbsp (12g) all-purpose flour

1 cup Guinness draught

Optional: Finely chopped Italian parsley for garnishment

Umami Chicken Stock Mixture

½ cup unsalted homemade chicken stock

1 tbsp Worcestershire sauce

1 tbsp light soy sauce (not low sodium soy sauce)

1 tbsp fish sauce

1 tbsp tomato paste

Simple Mashed Potatoes:

6 Yukon gold potatoes (halved)

100 ml whole milk

1 - 2 tbsp (14g-28g) unsalted butter

Kosher salt & pepper to taste

How You Make It:

1. Preheat your instant pot using the saute function.

2. While on that, season the chuck steak with kosher salt and pepper.

3. Pour 1 tbsp olive oil into the instant pot and brown the chuck steak in it for 6 - 8 mins on each side without flipping. When done, remove and set aside.

4. Meanwhile, make the Umami Chicken Stock Mixture by mixing 1 tbsp Worcestershire sauce with 1 tbsp light soy sauce, 1 tbsp fish sauce, 1 tbsp tomato paste and ½ cup unsalted homemade chicken stock.

5. Next, add 1 tbsp of olive oil to the IP and saute the veggies in it for 1 min (onions & shallots). Add the minced garlic cloves and stir for roughly 30 secs or until fragrant.

6. Include the quartered mushrooms and sauté for another 3 mins, then Season with salt and ground black pepper.

7. Now, deglaze by pouring in ½ cup Guinness draught and scrubbing the flavorful brown bits with wooden spoon. When done, pour in the rest.

8. At this point, add 1 bay leaf, 2 sprigs thyme, dark chocolate, russet potato chunks, 1 sprig rosemary, carrot chunks and chicken stock mixture in the pot.

9. Mix well, and secure the lid. Pressure cook at High for 4 mins (use Quick Release and open the lid)

10. Now, cut the chuck steak into 2 inches stew cubes and place in a large missing bowl. Add 1.5 tbsp flour in the mixing bowl and mix with the stew meat.

11. With the help of a spoon, remove half of the carrot chunks and all mushrooms the cooker: set aside.

12. Place all beef stew meat and its juice in the IP without stirring. Layer a stainless-steel bowl filled with halved potatoes on top.

13. Secure the lid and pressure cook at High Pressure for 32 mins (use 10 mins Natural Release +quick release).

14. Open the lid and remove the bowl.

15. Discard the bay leaf and the herbs. press Sauté, break down the mushy russet potatoes with wooden spoon and stir to thicken the stew. Return the sautéed mushrooms and carrots in the pot. Taste and season with salt and pepper if needed.

16. Finally, mash the cooked potatoes in a bowl with a potato masher. Mix in 100ml whole milk and 2 tbsp unsalted butter. Season with salt & pepper as needed and serve stew over mashed potatoes, garnished with Italian Parsley.

Cauliflower Potato Soup

Prep: 10 mins

Cook: 30 mins

Total: 40 mins

Serving: 4 - 6

Ingredients

1 head of cauliflower, floret

2 small red potatoes (chunked)

6 cloves of garlic (minced)

1 cup of heavy cream

4 cups of unsalted homemade chicken stock

6 slices of bacon (chopped)

1 medium onion (diced)

2 bay leaves

2 stalks of green onions (chopped)

2 tbsp fish sauce (optional)

freshly grated Parmesan cheese (optional for garnish)

How You Make It:

1. First, place the chopped bacon in your instant pot and saute until crisp (4 mins).

2. When done, remove the bacon bits and place on a paper towel to absorb fats.

3. Throw the onion into the instant pot and sauté alongside the Garlic, and Green onions (1 – 2 mins or until soften).

4. Once that is achieved, pour in ⅓ cup stock. With the help of a wooden spoon, scrub all the brown bits off the cooker bottom.

5. Add bay leaves, cauliflower, potatoes and remaining stock into the IP. Secure the lid and cook at High Pressure for 3 mins. (Use 10 mins Natural Release + quick release).

6. Open the lid carefully and discard the bay Leaves. Blend cauliflower soup into desired consistency with the help of an immersion hand blender.

7. Add 1 cup of heavy cream. Taste and season with 2 tbsp of fish sauce and salt.

8. When done, serve garnished with green onions, bacon bits from step 2, and freshly grated Parmesan cheese.

Italian Chicken Soup

8 servings

245 cals

Prep time: 25 m

Cook time: 25 m

Ready In 50 m

Ingredients

2 tsp olive oil

4 Italian turkey sausage links (casings removed)

3 cloves garlic (minced)

1 cup green lentils

3 cups chicken stock

1 medium onion (diced)

½ cup pearl barley

1 bone-in chicken breast half (skin removed)

½ cup chopped fresh parsley

1 (15 oz.) can chickpeas (garbanzo beans) (drained)

1 (16 oz.) bag fresh spinach leaves (chopped)

1 cup mild salsa

How You Make It:

1. First, heat 1 tsp of olive oil in the IP using the saute function.

2. Brown the sausage meat in the oil, breaking it into crumbles. When done, take out the sausage.

3. Add another 1 tsp of olive oil to cooker and saute the onion and garlic in it until onion is transparent.

4. Include barley. Stir for 1 minute and return sausage to cooker.

5. Now, add lentils, chicken, parsley, and stock to cooker. The chicken stock should be enough to cover the chicken.

6. Secure the lid and push the pressure cook button. Cook for 10 mins at high pressure (use quick-release).

7. Carefully open the cooker and remove chicken. Shred once cool enough to handle and return to soup.

8. Add the garbanzo beans, spinach and salsa.

9. Finally, stir well to blend and heat through before serving.

Stew Beef Sauerbraten

Servings: 4
Cals: 764
Prep time: 20 m
Cook time: 20 m
Ready In: 40 m

Ingredients

2 tbsp shortening

2 lbs cubed beef stew meat

1 cup white vinegar

1 tsp browning sauce

salt & pepper to taste

5 cups water

3 bay leaves

½ cup water

2 tbsp all-purpose flour

How You Make It:

1. First, melt the shortening in your instant pot electric pressure cooker using the saute function.

2. After that, add the stew beef, and cook, turning occasionally, until browned.

3. Next, you pour in the water, browning sauce and vinegar. Include the bay leaves and season with salt and pepper to taste.

4. Secure the lid. Select pressure cook and cook for 17 mins at high pressure (use 10 mins natural release + quick release).

5. Meanwhile, mix the flour with ½ cup of water and pour into the cooker.

6. Push the saute button and cook, stirring frequently, until thickened.

Caveman Stew

Servings: 4

481 cals

Prep time: 10 m

Cook time: 20 m

Ready In: 30 m

Ingredients

1 pound ground beef

5 carrots (sliced)

4 potatoes (cut into quarters)

1 onion (quartered)

1 (10.75 oz.) can condensed tomato soup

1 (10.75 oz.) can water

How You Make It:

1. First, shape the ground beef into 6 meatballs.

2. Next, mix the carrots, potatoes, and onion together in your instant pot and arrange the meatballs on it.

3. When done, pour in the tomato soup and water. Secure the lid.

4. Select pressure cook and cook for 17 mins at high pressure. (use 10 mins natural release + quick release).

CHAPTER 5: BEANS & GRAIN

Potato Risotto

Serves 4 to 6

Ingredients:

1 tbsp olive oil

1 medium yellow onion (chopped)

1 medium golden, red, or new potato (chopped into ½ -inch cubes)

1 tbsp tomato paste

2 cups Arborio (or any short-grain rice)

¼ cup white wine (a tart wine, such as pinot grigio or chardonnay)

4 cups salt-free vegetable stock

1 ½ tsp salt (withhold if using purchased stock)

A few sprigs of thyme

How You Make It:

1. Preheat the IP using the saute function and add the olive oil.

2. Saute the onion until it softens and add rice. Stir constantly for about 5 mins and add the wine.

3. Stir constantly until the rice absorbs all of the wine and then, include the potatoes, stock, tomato paste, and salt.

4. Secure the lid. Select pressure-cook and cook for 5 mins at high pressure (use quick release).

5. Open the lid, give the content a good stir and serve sprinkled with fresh thyme.

Penne Rigate Pasta

Prep: 5 mins

Cook: 20 mins

Total: 25 mins

Serving: 2 - 4

Ingredients

450 grams penne pasta

1 small shallot (diced) (optional)

12 white mushrooms (sliced)

1 small onion (sliced)

3 cloves garlic (minced)

1 zucchini squash (sliced)

A dash of sherry wine

A pinch of dried basil

A pinch of dried oregano

Kosher salt and black pepper to taste

Olive oil

Pasta Sauce:

1 cup unsalted homemade chicken stock (or vegetable stock + 2 cups water)

156 ml (5.5 fl oz can) tomato paste

2 tbsp light soy sauce (not low sodium soy sauce)

1 tbsp Worcestershire sauce

1 tbsp fish sauce

How You Make It:

1. First, preheat your instant pot using the saute function.

2. Sauté sliced zucchini squash in it with 1 tbsp of olive oil and set aside.

3. Pour in 1 tbsp of olive oil. Add onion to cooker and saute alongside the garlic, and Shallot.

4. Include a pinch of kosher salt and ground black pepper. Stir occasionally until slightly browned.

5. Once that is achieved, add sliced mushrooms, dried oregano, and basil.

6. Cook for one minute and taste. Adjust if necessary.

7. Now, pour in a dash of sherry wine and scrub the cooker bottom with a wooden spoon.

8. At this point, pour the chicken stock (or vegetable stock), water, soy sauce, fish sauce, and Worcestershire sauce in the cooker and mix well.

9. Pour Penne in the sauce and place the tomato paste on top of the pasta.

10. You can now mix and again, taste for seasoning. Make sure the Penne are completely submerged in the sauce and secure the lid.

11. Select pressure cook and cook for 5 mins at high pressure. (use 5 mins natural release + quick release).

12. Serve immediately.

Fennel Soup II

Prep time: 10 m
Cook time: 15 m
Ready In: 25 m

Ingredients

1 fennel bulb (diced)
1 bay leaf
1 tbsp olive oil
1 small leek (sliced)
½ cube vegetable bouillon
2 cups water
2 tsp grated Parmesan cheese

How You Make It:

1. Add the fennel, bay leaf, leek, vegetable bouillon, and water to the instant pot duo plus or any other electric pressure cooker and secure the lid.

2. Select pressure cook and cook for 17 mins at high pressure. (quick release).

3. Add the olive oil and sprinkle with Parmesan cheese

4. Serve.

Pasta Bolognese

Prep: 5 mins
Cook: 25 mins
Total: 30 mins
Serving: 4

Ingredients

½ pound ground beef

450 grams (16oz) penne rigate

3 cloves garlic (minced)

12 white mushrooms (sliced)

1 celery (chopped)

A pinch of dried oregano

1 small onion (sliced)

A dash of sherry wine

A pinch of dried basil

Kosher salt and black pepper to taste

Olive oil

Pasta Sauce:

1 cup unsalted homemade chicken stock (+ 2 cups water)

156 ml (5.5 fl oz can) tomato paste

2 tbsp light soy sauce (not low sodium soy sauce)

1 tbsp fish sauce

1 tbsp Worcestershire sauce

How You Make It:

1. Preheat your instant pot duo plus or any other instant pot model using by tapping the saute button twice.

2. Once hot, add 1 tbsp of oil to it. Season the ground beef with salt and ground black pepper. Brown on all sides and set aside.

3. Add 1 tbsp of oil to cooker and sauté the onion it with a pinch of kosher salt and ground black pepper.

4. Once the onion looks slightly browned, add minced garlic and stir for about 30 seconds or until fragrant.

5. Throw in the sliced mushrooms, celery, oregano, and basil. Cook this for another minute and taste for seasoning. Adjust as needed.

6. At this point, pour in a dash of sherry wine. Scrub the cooker bottom with a wooden spoon and return ground beef.

7. Pour in the chicken stock, water, light soy sauce, fish sauce, and Worcestershire sauce. Mix well.

8. Add pasta, tomato paste and secure the lid. Pressure cook at High Pressure for 4 mins. (5 mins natural + quick pressure release when done).

9. Serve sprinkled with some freshly grated Parmesan cheese.

Jamaican Oxtail with Broad Beans

Prep time: 30 m

Cook time: 45 m

Ready In: 1 h 15 m

4 servings

425 cals

Ingredients

1 pound beef oxtail (cut into pieces)

1 large onion (chopped)

2 cloves garlic (minced)

1 green onion (sliced)

1 scotch bonnet chile pepper (chopped)

½ tsp salt

1 ½ cups water

1 tsp minced fresh ginger root

2 tbsp soy sauce

1 sprig fresh thyme (chopped)

1 tsp black pepper

2 tbsp vegetable oil

1 cup canned fava beans (drained)

1 tsp whole allspice berries

1 tbsp cornstarch

2 tbsp water

How You Make It:

1. First, toss the oxtail with garlic, onion, green onion, chile pepper, ginger, soy sauce, thyme, salt, and pepper.

2. Place a skillet over medium-heat. Heat the vegetable oil in and brown the oxtail all over (takes 10 mins).

3. When done, place into your instant pot electric pressure cooker and pour in the water.

4. Cook at high pressure for 25 mins. (Use quick release).

5. Now, add the fava beans and allspice berries. Bring to a simmer using the saute setting at "Medium".

6. At this point, mix the cornstarch in 2 tbsp water and stir into pot.

7. Cook, stir until the sauce has thickened, and the beans are tender.

Rajma (Kidney Bean Curry)

Prep time: 10 m

Cook time: 1 h

Ready In: 1 h 10 m

Ingredients

2 cups dry red kidney beans (soaked for 8 hrs. or overnight)

1 large onion (chopped)

4 cloves garlic (chopped)

1 (2 inch) piece fresh ginger root (chopped)

2 tsp ghee (clarified butter)

2 dried red chile peppers (broken into pieces)

1 tsp cumin seeds

1 tsp ground turmeric

2 tbsp vegetable oil

6 whole cloves

2 tomatoes (chopped)

2 tsp garam masala

1 tsp ground cumin

1 tsp ground coriander

2 cups water

1 tsp white sugar

salt to taste

1 tsp ground red pepper

¼ cup cilantro leaves (chopped)

How You Make It:

1. First, with the help of a mortar, grind the onion, ginger, and garlic into a paste.

2. Next, heat the oil and ghee together in your instant pot using the saute function.

3. Saute the red chile peppers, cumin seeds, and cloves in it until the cumin seeds begin to splutter.

4. Once that is achieved, stir the onion paste into the mixture and cook, stir, until golden brown.

5. Now, add the ground turmeric, ground cumin, and ground coriander. Cook for a few more seconds and include the tomatoes: cook this until the tomatoes are completely tender.

6. Drain and rinse the beans. Add to cooker with enough water to cover and include the sugar and salt.

7. Secure the lid. pressure cook for 15 mins at high (use quick release).

8. Open cooker and stir in the masala and ground red pepper.

9. Serve garnished with chopped cilantro to serve.

CHAPTER 6: BEEF, PORK & LAMB

Beef Curry

4 servings

Ingredients:

2 tomatoes (cut into quarters)

1 small onion (cut into quarters)

4 garlic cloves (peeled & chopped)

1 tsp ground cumin

½ tsp ground coriander

½ tsp ground cayenne pepper

½ cup fresh cilantro

1 tsp Garam Masala

1 tsp salt (+more for seasoning)

1 pound beef chuck roast (cut into 1-inch cubes)

How You Make It:

1. First, blend the tomatoes, onion, garlic, and cilantro together until puree with a blender.

2. Next, you add and process the cumin, coriander, garam masala, cayenne, and salt.

3. Add the beef to your instant pot and pour the vegetable puree on top.

4. Secure the IP lid and pressure cook at high for 20 minutes (use 10 mins natural release + quick release).

5. Open the lid. Stir in the curry. Taste and adjust seasoning, and serve with naan.

Texas Venison

Prep time: 25 m

Cook time: 15 m

Ready In: 1 h

4 servings

492 cals

Ingredients

2 pounds venison steaks

1 cup all-purpose flour

½ tsp ground cumin

2 beef bouillon cubes

1 ½ tsp seasoned salt (divided)

4 tbsp vegetable oil

½ cup onion (halved & sliced)

½ tsp dried Mexican oregano

1 bay leaf

2 dried red chile peppers (whole with stems removed)

2 cups water

How You Make It:

1. First, lightly season the venison steaks with Salt and cut into bite-sized pieces.

2. Next, mix the flour with 1 tsp of salt (after mixing, RESERVE 1 tbsp) and toss with the cubed meat.

3. After that, heat the oil in the instant pot using the saute function and add the meat cubes in batches. Cook this until richly browned on all sides: set aside.

4. When done, reduce the saute heat to medium. Stir the reserved flour and the ground cumin into the pan drippings.

5. Continue cooking and stirring until the flour has lost its raw smell (about 5 mins).

6. Now, add the sliced onion and cook, stir until the onion has softened (takes about 5 mins).

7. At this point, return the meat to the pan, along with the Mexican oregano, beef bouillon cubes, bay leaf, and chile peppers.

8. Pour in the water and close the lid. Pressure Cook at high pressure for 15 mins (Use natural release).

9. Open the lid. remove the chile peppers and bay leaf. Hold and squeeze the pulp from the peppers. After that, return the pulp to the pan and discard the skins along with the bay leaf.

10. Taste and adjust the seasonings. Then serve!

Pork Tenderloin

8 h 40 m 6 servings 151 cals

Prep time: 15 m
Cook time: 25 m
Ready In: 8 h 40 m

Ingredients

¼ cup fresh cilantro leaves

¼ cup lime juice

¼ cup olive oil

½ tsp red pepper flakes, or to taste

¾ cup chicken broth

2 cloves garlic (sliced)

¼ tsp salt (or to taste)

1 pound pork tenderloin

¼ cup lemon juice

How You Make It:

1. First, blend the cilantro, lime juice, garlic, olive oil, red pepper flakes, and salt until smooth in a blender. Pour into a large resealable plastic bag when done.

2. Next, add the pork tenderloin to the plastic bag and manipulate to get it covered with the marinade.

3. Seal and marinate in refrigerator for 8 hours or overnight.

4. After that, stir the chicken broth and lemon juice in your instant pot duo plus or any IP model and lay the tenderloin into the liquid.

5. Pour the remaining marinade on the tenderloin and close the lid.

6. Pressure cooker and cook for 28 mins at high pressure (use 5 mins natural release + quick release).

7. When done, slice the tenderloin into medallions and serve.

Shredded Pork Taco Filling

Prep time: 10 m

Cook time: 45 m

Ready In: 1 h 15 m

6 servings

363 cals

Ingredients

½ tsp garlic powder

2 tsp ground coriander

2 tsp ground cumin

2 tsp dried oregano

4 cups beef broth

¼ tsp cayenne pepper

1 (3 ½) pound pork shoulder roast

2 bay leaves

½ large white onion (cut into large chunks)

How You Make It:

1. Simply combine the garlic powder with the cumin, coriander, oregano, and cayenne pepper in a bowl.

2. After combining, thoroughly rub the mixture over pork.

3. When done, place the roast in your instant pot and pour in the beef broth, bay leaves, and onion.

4. Secure the lid. Cook at high pressure for 45 mins (Use natural release).

5. Carefully open the lid and transfer the pork to a dish.

6. Shred and serve.

Greek Style Beef Stew

Prep time: 35 m

Cook time: 15 m

Ready In:1 h 10 m

6 servings

289 cals

Ingredients

1 tbsp olive oil

1 pound cubed beef stew meat

1 large clove garlic (minced)

1 onion (peeled & chopped)

2 tbsp red wine vinegar

½ tsp dried oregano

1 tsp ground cumin

1 ½ tsp light brown sugar

¼ cup red wine

½ cup fat-free reduced-sodium beef broth

1 tbsp tomato paste

½ tsp dried rosemary

6 whole black peppercorns

2 bay leaves

1/8 tsp ground cinnamon

1 pinch ground cloves

¼ tsp ground black pepper

1 (28 oz.) can whole plum tomatoes (undrained & quartered)

½ cup water

2 potatoes (peeled & cut into 2-inch pieces)

2 carrots (peeled & sliced)

salt to taste (optional)

How You Make It:

1. Preheat your instant pot using the saute function and add the olive oil.

2. Once hot, add half the beef and saute until well browned on all sides. Remove and brown the rest: set aside.

3. Next, place the chopped onion in the cooker and cook-stir for 1 minute. Throw in the garlic and stir for an additional minute.

4. After that, pour in the red wine, red wine vinegar, broth and tomato paste: mix well.

5. With the help of a mortar, crush the rosemary, oregano, and peppercorns. Add this to cooker along with cumin, cinnamon, bay leaves, cloves, black pepper, and brown sugar.

6. At this point, pour in tomatoes, potatoes, carrots, and browned meat.

7. Close the lid and select pressure cook. Cook for 15 mins at high (use 10 mins natural + quick release).

8. Taste the stew and add salt, if desired.

Mensaf (Jordanian Lamb Stew)

Prep time: 15 m

Cook time: 55 m

Ready In: 1 h 10 m

8 servings

544 cals

Ingredients

4 tbsp olive oil

2 pounds boneless lamb shoulder (cut into 2 inch pieces)

2 cups uncooked white rice

6 pita bread rounds

8 cups water

¼ cup pine nuts

1 cup salted goat's milk (jameed el-kasih)

How You Make It:

1. Select saute in your instant pot duo plus or any other model of the instant pot and add 1 tbsp olive oil to it.

2. Once hot, add the lamb and cook until browned on all sides. Set aside and insert a cooking rack into the instant pot.

3. Place the browned lamb on the rack and pour in 4 cups water.

4. Secure the lid. Cook for 45 mins at high pressure (Use natural release).

5. Carefully open the lid and remove lamb. Discard the bones and pour broth into a bowl: set aside.

6. Place a sauce pan over medium-high heat. Add remaining four cups of water, 1 tbsp olive oil, and the rice in it and bring to a boil.

7. Reduce heat and simmer until all moisture is absorbed (takes 20 mins).

8. Now, place a skillet over medium heat and add the remaining 2 tbsp olive oil to it. Cook, stir the pine nuts in it until deep brown (took about 5 mins).

9. Once that is achieved, pour 2 cups of the broth from step 5 into a large pan and pour in the goat's milk. Add the lamb and simmer over medium heat for about 30 mins.

10. When done, serve (simply place the pita bread in a large platter. Spoon rice over bread and place the lamb on top. Drizzle with any remaining milk mixture, and finally, sprinkle with pine nuts).

CHAPTER 7: FISH/SEAFOOD RECIPES

Shrimp Paella

Prep Time 10 mins

Cook Time 5 mins

Total Time 15 mins

Servings 4

Calories 318 kcal

Ingredients

1 lb jumbo shrimp, shell and tail on frozen

1 cup Jasmine rice

4 Tbsp butter

1 onion chopped

4 cloves garlic chopped

1 red pepper chopped

1 cup chicken broth

1/2 cup white wine

1 tsp paprika

1 tsp turmeric

1/2 tsp salt

1/4 tsp black pepper

1 pinch saffron threads

1/4 tsp red pepper flakes

1/4 cup cilantro optional

How You Make It:

1. Select saute in your Instant Pot and melt the butter in it.

2. Cook the onion until softened and add garlic: cook for one more mins and add paprika, turmeric, red pepper flakes, salt, black pepper, and saffron threads.

3. Stir, cook for a minute and add the red peppers.

4. Next, add rice and stir. Pour in the chicken broth and white wine to cover the rice.

5. Place the shrimp on top and secure the lid. Cook for 5 minutes at high pressure and use the quick release method.

6. Carefully open the lid and remove shrimp. Peel if desired and serve with Cilantro.

Cajun Shrimp and Sausage Boil

Prep Time: 10 mins

Cook Time: 10 mins

Total Time: 20 mins

Ingredients

½ pounds smoked sausage (cut into four pieces)

1 tbsp Louisiana Shrimp & Crab Boil

4 ears corn

2 red potatoes (cut in half)

Water to cover the above

½ pounds raw shrimp

For sauce

6 tbsp butter

1/8 tsp cajun seasoning

1 tbsp garlic (minced)

¼ tsp Old Bay seasoning

3-5 shakes hot sauce, such as Louisiana Hot sauce or Tabasco

1/8 tsp lemon pepper

½ lemon, juiced

How You Make It:

1. First, add all the first set of ingredients (except shrimp) and close the lid.

2. Cook at High pressure for 4 mins (use quick release).

3. Melt the butter in a pan over medium-high heat and add the minced garlic. Sauté for a few mins and add all other spices.

4. Mix well to combine and set aside.

5. Open the instant pot and add the shrimp. Once it turns pink, take them out, along with the corn, potatoes, and sausage.

6. Now put everything into the sauce, and stir well to coat with the spiced butter goodness.

7. Serve immediately.

Chickpeas with Eel

Ingredients

400 grams chickpeas (soaked overnight)

100 grams smoked eel (dried) (soaked overnight in a separate bowl)

200 grams spinach

1 onions

1 piece bread

extra-virgin olive oil

1 leeks

1 bay leaf

5 quail eggs

Salt to taste

How You Make It:

1. First, add the chickpeas, onion, leek, and bay leaf in your instant pot and seal the lid.

2. Cook the chickpeas for 20 mins (quick release when done).

3. Meanwhile, drain and chop eel.

4. Open the cooker and remove the onion and leek.

5. Add chopped eel and cook for 15 mins using the saute function.

6. Add oil in a small saucepan and heat over medium-high. Fry a slice of bread in the oil.

7. Combine the fried bread with the leek and onion then grind.

8. Mix with chickpeas in cooker.

9. Boil quail eggs.

10. Once the chickpeas are done, stir in the spinach and cook for 2 more mins.

11. Divide into plates and serve garnished with quail egg.

CHAPTER 8: CHICKEN/POULTRY

Fricase de Pollo

Prep time: 25 m

Cook time: 15 m

Ready In: 1 h

Servings

454 cals

Ingredients

1 tbsp extra-virgin olive oil

½ large red bell pepper (diced)

4 cloves garlic (smashed)

2 tbsp tomato paste

½ red onion (diced)

2 cups water (or as needed)

6 skinless chicken leg quarters (separated into thighs & drumsticks)

salt to taste

How You Make It:

1. Preheat the instant pot using the saute function and add olive oil. Stir in red bell pepper and onion.

2. Cook, stir until the onion has softened (about 5 mins). Add garlic and cook until golden.

3. Once that is achieved, dissolve tomato paste in 1 cup of water and stir into cooker.

4. Next, place chicken and add enough water so its nearly covered.

5. Secure the lid and cook at high pressure for 17 mins (use 20 mins natural release).

6. Open the lid and season chicken with salt to taste. Could be served with black beans and rice

Cacciatore Chicken

Serves 4 to 6

Ingredients

1 cup salt-free chicken stock

6 to 8 bone-in chicken drumsticks (or a mix of drumsticks and thighs)

1 tsp dried oregano

1 tsp salt (omit this if using salted stock)

1 bay leaf

1 medium yellow onion (chopped)

1 tsp garlic powder

1 (28-oz.) can whole stewed tomatoes in purée

½ cup black olives (about 2.5 oz.) (pitted)

How You Make It:

1. First, preheat the instant pot using the saute function.

2. Pour in the chicken stock, salt, and bay leaf. Mix well, and add in the following order the chicken, onion, garlic powder, oregano, and tomatoes.

3. Seal the lid and cook at high pressure for 15 mins (use 5 mins natural + quick release).

4. Open the lid and stir the content. Discard the bay leaf.

5. Arrange the chicken and tomatoes on a platter and drizzle with cooking liquid.

6. Sprinkle with black olives before serving.

7. You can also reduce the cooking liquid to a desired consistency and serve over chicken and pasta.

Chicken Salad

Prep Time: 5 mins
Cook Time: 20 mins
Total Time: 25 mins
Servings: 2

Ingredients

Chicken Breast

1 (300 grams) (amounts to 2/3 pound) boneless, skinless chicken breast
1 cup water

Brine

2 cups water
30 grams salt

Honey Mustard Vinaigrette Salad Dressing

3 cloves garlic (minced)
1 tbsp dijon mustard
A pinch of kosher salt
1 tbsp honey
1 tbsp balsamic vinegar
3 tbsp extra virgin olive oil

Salad

Field greens
Grape tomatoes (cut in half)

How You Make It:

1. First, add 30g of salt and 2 cups of water into a mixing bowl and mix well. Place the chicken breast in the mixture and refrigerate for 45 mins.

2. After that, pour 1 cup of water into the instant pot and insert the cooking rack. Place chicken the rack and seal the lid.

3. Cook at High Pressure for 5 mins (use 10 mins natural release + quick release)

4. Open the lid. Transfer chicken to plate.

5. Meanwhile add 3 cloves of finely minced garlic in a bowl along with 1 tbsp of Dijon mustard, 1 tbsp of balsamic vinegar and 1 tbsp of honey.

6. Gently mix with a spoon and pour in 3 tbsp of extra virgin olive oil. Continue mixing until emulsified.

7. Once that is achieved, slice chicken breast uniformly and place them on the field greens and grape tomatoes.

8. Finally, drizzle with honey mustard vinaigrette on top and serve.

BBQ Chicken Wings

Prep: 5 mins

Cook: 30 mins

Total: 35 mins

Serving: 2 - 3

Ingredients

2 pounds chicken wings & drumettes

½ cup Sweet Baby Ray's Original BBQ Sauce

How You Make It:

1. First, pour 1 cup of water into your instant pot and insert a steamer basket.

2. Add the wings and drumettes on the basket and seal the lid.

3. Cook at High Pressure for 5 mins + Full Natural Release.

4. Now, preheat your Air fryer to 400°F and set the timer to 10 mins. If using an oven, preheat the oven to 450°F.

5. Pat the wings and drumettes dry with paper towels.

6. Toss the wings and drumettes with the BBQ sauce and put them in the air fryer basket.

7. Allow to Air fry until sauce is glossy and caramelized (takes about 5–10 mins).

8. Again, if using an oven, place the wings and drumettes in a single layer on a wire rack inside a baking tray: bake for 8 to 15 minutes or until the sauce is glossy and caramelized.

General Tso's Chicken

Prep: 5 mins

Cook: 40 mins

Total: 45 mins

Serving: 2 - 4

Ingredients

8 - 10 chicken drumsticks

1 -2 stalks green onion (with green part finely chopped for garnish and the white part cut into 1.5 inch pieces)

3 garlic cloves (minced)

1 tbsp peanut oil

10 dried Chinese red chili

1 (10g) slice ginger (chopped)

1 tbsp honey (Optional)

General Tso's Sauce:

¼ cup dark soy sauce

2 tbsp Chinese black vinegar or distilled white vinegar

2 tbsp Shaoxing wine

¼ cup sugar

1 tsp sesame oil

Thickener:

2 tbsp cornstarch + 2 tbsp water

Serving:

16-20 pieces lettuce

Optional: Hoisin sauce

How You Make It:

1. Preheat your instant pot using the saute function and add 1 tbsp peanut oil.

2. Once oil gets hot, add Chinese red chili, minced garlic, green onions white part, and chopped ginger. Sauté for roughly 3 mins.

3. Add all the sauce mixture to cooker along with the chicken drumsticks. Secure the lid.

4. Pressure cook at High Pressure for 12 mins (Use 12 mins Natural Release + quick release).

5. Open the lid carefully. Take out the drumsticks and shred separating from the bones.

6. Remove the Chinese red chili and select saute. Bring the sauce back to a boil. Add 1 tbsp of honey to sweeten (if desired).

7. At this point, mix cornstarch with water and slowly stir into pot.

8. Return shredded chicken to pot and mix well.

9. To serve, place pulled chicken onto lettuce and garnish with the finely chopped green onion. Could be served with Hoisin Sauce on the side.

Cola Chicken Wings

Prep: 5 mins

Cook: 25 mins

Total: 30 mins

Serving: 2 - 4

Ingredients

1 ½ pound chicken wings

1 stalk green onion (cut 2 inches long)

200 ml regular coca cola

4 cloves garlic (crushed)

1 tbsp ginger (sliced)

1 tbsp dark soy sauce

2 tbsp light soy sauce (not low sodium soy sauce)

1 tbsp Chinese rice wine

1 tbsp peanut oil

How You Make It:

1. Preheat your instant pot using the saute function and add the peanut oil.

2. Saute the crushed garlic, sliced ginger and green onions in the oil for a minute or until fragrant.

3. Once achieved, add the chicken wings and stir fry in the garlic mixture for 1 to 2 mins.

4. When the begins to brown, pour in the coca cola. Deglaze the cooker bottom with the help of a wooden spoon.

5. After that, add light soy sauce, dark soy sauce, and Chinese rice wine. Mix well and seal the lid.

6. Pressure Cook at High Pressure for 5 mins (Use 10 mins natural + quick release).

7. Open the lid, select saute and reduce to a desired consistency.

8. Serve immediately with rice.

Filipino Chicken Adobo

Prep: 10 mins

Cook: 25 mins

Total: 35 mins

Serving: 2 - 4

Ingredients

6 chicken drumsticks or 2 pounds chicken meat

1 tbsp oil

Green onions (chopped for garnish)

Sauce

¼ cup Filipino soy sauce

¼ cup Filipino vinegar

1 tbsp sugar

½ cup light soy sauce (not low sodium soy sauce)

1 tbsp fish sauce

1 small onion (minced)

4 dried bay leaves

10 cloves garlic (crushed)

1 tsp ground black peppercorn

1 dried red chili

1 tsp cornstarch + 1 tbsp water (optional)

How You Make It:

1. Take out a medium mixing bowl and combine the Filipino soy sauce, light soy sauce, fish sauce, Filipino vinegar, and sugar.

2. After that, add oil to the instant pot and brown the chicken for 1 to 2 mins using the saute function. Remove when done.

3. Add garlic and onion to pot and saute until fragrant and golden in color.

4. Include the ground black peppercorn, red chili, and bay leaves. Sauté for 30 seconds and add the Sauce mixture.

5. Stir the cooker bottom and return drumsticks to pot.

6. Secure the lid and cook at high pressure for 9 mins (use natural release).

7. Now to thicken, remove the chicken and simmer the sauce. Mix cornstarch with water and slowly stir into pot.

8. You can also brown the chicken in a broiler for 5 mins.

9. Serve chicken in plates with the sauce alongside chopped green onions for garnish.

Soy Sauce Chicken and Rice

Prep: 5 mins

Cook: 30 mins

Total: 35 mins

Serving: 2 - 4

Ingredients

8 bone-in chicken legs

1 tbsp dark soy sauce

Master Stock Mixture

3 tbsp light soy sauce (not low sodium soy sauce)

½ tbsp dark soy sauce

4 garlic cloves (crushed)

3 star anise

½ tsp Sichuan pepper

¾ cup water

Rice

1 cup jasmine rice

1 cup water

How You Make It:

1. First, add light soy sauce, ½ tbsp dark soy sauce, garlic cloves, Sichuan pepper, star anise, and ¾ cup water to your instant pot and stir to mix.

2. Place the chicken in the IP as well and insert a tall steamer rack. Add the rice with 1 cup of water in a stainless steel bowl and place it on the rack.

3. Close lid and pressure cook at High Pressure for 8 mins (Use 10 mins Natural + quick release).

4. When done, fluff & set aside the cooked rice and rack.

5. Take out a small mixing bowl and mix the 1 tbsp dark soy sauce with 1 tbsp Master Stock Mixture in pot and apply this on the chicken legs for additional color and flavor.

6. Serve over rice with your favorite vegetables.

CHAPTER 9: GLUTEN FREE, VEGETARIAN & KETO DIETS

Instant Pot Vegetable Soup (VG, V)

Any blend of vegetables you like can be used including fresh. I just like the ease and convenience of frozen ones.

Prep Time 5 minutes

Cook Time 40 minutes

Total Time 45 minutes

Servings 6

Calories 201 kcal

Ingredients

12 oz. frozen California vegetables

1 (15- oz) can diced tomatoes fire roasted preferred

12 oz. frozen Italian vegetables

1 15- oz can pinto beans, kidney beans (or your favorite beans undrained)

1 tbsp garlic minced

½ tsp salt

1 (15- oz) can cannelloni beans (or other white beans undrained)

¼ cup quinoa (rinsed)

1 tbsp dried basil

1 tbsp hot sauce

½ tbsp dried oregano

1 tsp onion powder

¼ tsp ground black pepper

3 cups boiling water

How You Make It:

1. Add all ingredients to your instant pot duo plus or any other brand and stir well to mix.

2. Close the lid and cook at High Pressure for 2 minutes (use quick release).

3. Open the lid and stir the soup.

Mega Veggie Chili (VG, V)

Prep Time 10 minutes

Cook Time 30 minutes

Total Time 40 minutes

Servings 6

Calories 228 kcal

Ingredients

1 large onion (chopped)

2 carrots (diced)

2 bell peppers (chopped into ½ -inch pieces)

2 ribs celery (sliced)

4 cloves garlic (minced)

1 tsp ground cumin

2 15-oz cans cooked beans (pinto, kidney, or combination), drained

2 cups fresh or frozen corn (thawed)

1 jalapeno chile seeds removed & diced)

1 tbsp mild chili powder

¼ tsp chipotle chile powder (or to taste)

½ tsp salt (or to taste)

1 ½ cups water

1 (15-oz) can diced tomatoes (fire-roasted preferred)

½ cup medium grain bulgur wheat

additional seasonings to taste

lime wedges, jalapeño peppers, and fresh salsa to serve

How You Make It:

1. Preheat the instant pot using the saute function and add the garlic, onion and peppers.

2. Cook until the onion begins to soften, (takes 5-6 minutes).

3. Add beans, seasonings, water, and tomatoes. Stir well to mix and close the lid.

4. Cook at high pressure for 3 minutes and use quick release.

5. Stir in the corn and wheat. Taste for seasoning and add more chili powder, cumin, chipotle powder, or salt to taste.

6. Select saute and reduce to less. Simmer until the bulgur wheat is cooked and the chili has thickened.

7. Stir and divide into bowls. Serve with lime wedges, hot peppers and salsa.

Polenta with Lemony Asparagus & Chickpeas (VG, V)

Prep Time 15 minutes

Cook Time 40 minutes

Total Time 55 minutes

Servings 4

Calories 276 kcal

Ingredients

Polenta

2 ¼ cups water

1 cup coarse polenta coarse grind (such as Bob's Red Mill, not instant polenta)

2 cups vegetable broth

2 tsp minced garlic

1 tsp dried basil

Chickpeas

½ medium onion (chopped)

1 ½ cups cooked chickpeas or canned (drained & rinsed)

2 cloves garlic (minced)

½ tsp dried basil

1 tsp lemon juice

½ cup vegetable broth

¼ tsp freshly ground black pepper

1 tsp lemon zest peel (freshly grated)

1 tsp arrowroot or cornstarch

¼ cup water

Asparagus

1 tsp lemon peel freshly grated

coarse or flaky salt (such as Maldon) to taste

12 ozs asparagus ends trimmed and stalks (cut into 1 ½ -inch pieces)

lemon juice to taste

4 tsp pine nuts lightly toasted

How You Make It:

1. Add 2 ¼ cups water and 2 cups vegetable broth to your instant pot and bring to a boil using the saute function.

2. Add the polenta, garlic and basil. Stir to mix and lock the lid in place.

3. Cook at high pressure for 5 minutes + natural release.

4. Meanwhile, sauté the onion in a pan until it begins to soften. Add the garlic, chickpeas and stir for a min.

5. Pour in the broth, basil, and pepper. After which you reduce heat to low and simmer for 5 minutes.

6. Include the lemon peel and juice. Mix the cornstarch or arrowroot with ¼ cup water and add to pan.

7. Continue cooking until slightly thickened: Keep warm.

8. At this point, bring a large pot of water to a boil. Add the asparagus and blanch for 2 minutes.

9. When done, drain and toss with a squeeze of fresh lemon juice, lemon zest, and salt to taste.

10. Finally, divide polenta into plates and top with the chickpeas and asparagus.

11. Sprinkle with toasted pine nuts and serve.

Herbed Polenta (VG, V)

Ingredients

4 ¼ cups water

2 tsp minced garlic

1 cup polenta

1 bay leaf

2 tsp chopped oregano

1 tsp salt

3 tbsp chopped basil

2 tbsp chopped Italian parsley

1 tsp chopped rosemary

How You Make It:

1. Add water to your instant pot and bring to a boil using the saute function.

2. Add polenta, garlic, salt, bay leaf, oregano and rosemary. Half of the basil and parsley.

3. Seal the lid. Cook for 5 minutes at high pressure (use 10 mins natural + quick release.

4. Open the lid and remove the bay leaf. Stir polenta and sprinkle with remaining herbs.

5. Serve!

Homemade Chili Beans (VG, V)

Prep Time 15 minutes

Cook Time 40 minutes

Total Time 55 minutes

Servings 8

Calories 215 kcal

Ingredients

1 pound dried pinto beans rinsed (picked over, & soaked)

3 cups water

2-3tsp chili powder may use all or part chipotle chili powder

1 medium onion (chopped)

2 cloves garlic (chopped)

2tsp oregano

½ tsp ground cumin

2 whole dried red chilies optional

2 tbsp tomato paste see tip below

salt to taste

1 green bell pepper (minced)

How You Make It:

1. First, drain the beans and add to the instant pot along with the water, onion, garlic, oregano, cumin, and chilies.

2. Close the lid. Cook for 5 minutes at high pressure and allow pressure to drop naturally.

3. Carefully open the lid and remove the chilies.

4. Add the rest ingredients and cook, uncovered, for 20-30 mins.

5. Adjust seasonings to taste and serve hot with fresh salsa.

Duo Plus Collard Greens (G.F)

Prep Time 5 minutes

Cook Time 25 minutes

Total Time 30 minutes

Servings 4

Calories 373 kcal

Ingredients

1 tbsp olive oil

1 smoked turkey leg

1 onion

3 cloves garlic

32 oz chicken broth 1 liter(We used gluten free - low sodium)

2 lb collard greens (chopped)

How You Make It:

1. Select saute in your Instant pot and add olive oil, garlic and onion. Cook for about 5 minutes.

2. Deglaze the cooker with a little chicken broth and add the collard greens.

3. Press and pack the collard greens down to the bottom and add the smoked turkey leg.

4. Pour in the gluten-free chicken broth and secure the lid.

5. Cook for 20 minutes at high pressure + quick release.

6. Open the lid, remove the turkey leg and cut the meat into chunks.

7. Serve with the collard greens, and a little hot sauce if desired.

PUMPKIN SOUP (GF, Paleo)

Making this pumpkin soup in the instant pot is very easy and takes little time. I think you'll love it.

Prep Time 10 minutes

Cook Time 30 minutes

Total Time 40 minutes

Servings 4

Calories 242 kcal

Ingredients

2.5 lb fresh pumpkin puree (1115 g fresh, not canned)

1 medium onion (chopped)

2 tbsp olive oil

1 tsp turmeric

sea salt to taste

½ cup full fat coconut milk 125mls

½ inch piece of root ginger (chopped)

2 tsp cumin

3 cloves garlic (chopped)

freshly ground black pepper to taste

3 cups gluten-free chicken broth

How You Make It:

1. First, pressure cook pumpkin with 1 cup of water for 15 minutes at high pressure and use quick release. Peel pumpkin and set aside.

2. Select saute, add onion and saute in a little olive oil.

3. Include the garlic, turmeric, ginger, cumin, salt and pepper and cook for a few seconds before adding chicken broth, coconut milk, and cooked pumpkin.

4. Secure the lid and pressure cook at high for 5 minutes (Use 10 mins natural + quick release).

5. Open the lid. Blend up the pumpkin soup with an immersion blender until smooth.

6. Taste for seasoning and add as needed.

7. You can serve hot with toasted pumpkin seeds and drizzle coconut milk on it.

Cauliflower & Cheesy Muffins (K)

15.7g protein

26.4g fat

13.3g net carbohydrates

Ingredients

1/2 cup of coconut flour

1 cup of shredded cheddar

1 cup of shredded mozzarella

1 Tbsp dried onion flakes

salt & black pepper to taste or ½ tsp each

1 oz. grated parmesan

1 tsp baking powder

2 cups of cauliflower florets

2 beaten eggs

1 tsp garlic powder

2 Tbsp minced jalapeno

3 Tbsp melted butter

How You Make It:

1. First, add all the ingredients in a bowl and stir well to combine.

2. Spray food release on silicone muffin cups and fill with batter.

3. Now, pour about 2 cups of water into the instant pot and fit in the steamer basket.

4. Carefully set the cups on the basket and lock the lid in place.

5.   Cook at high pressure for 20 minutes using the steam function and release pressure using the quick release method.

6.   Remove and serve.

IP Buffalo Ranch (K)

Prep time: 2 mins

Cook time: 15 mins

Total time: 17 mins

Ingredients

1-pound chicken breast

1 packet ranch dip

1 cup Hot Sauce

1 stick butter

8 oz cream cheese

16 oz cheddar cheese

How You Make It:

1. Add the first 5 ingredients to your Instant Pot and lock the lid in place.

2. Cook for 15 minutes on high pressure using the manual function and do a quick release.

3. Shred chicken with a fork or use your mixer to break it up.

4. Stir in cheddar cheese and serve with chips.

CHAPTER 10: INSTANT POT DUO PLUS SLOW COOKER RECIPES

Shredded Chicken

Could be placed in an airtight container and stored in the refrigerator for up to 4 days or in the freezer for up to 4 months.

Ingredients

4 large boneless, skinless chicken breasts

1 cup chicken stock (or water)

How You Make It:

1. Simply add the ingredients to your IP duo plus and close the lid.

2. Select slow cook and adjust time to either 5 hours on low, or 2 to 3 hours on high.

3. When done, shred the chicken and serve.

Ketchup

Makes 1 ½ to 2 cups

Ingredients

1 (28-oz.) can crushed tomatoes

½ cup apple cider vinegar

¼ cup packed brown sugar

½ small onion (diced)

2 tsp kosher salt

½ tsp celery seed

1 tsp paprika

½ tsp black pepper

Pinch ground allspice

What you need

Can opener

Chef's knife

Measuring cups

Cutting board

Measuring spoons

Your IP duo plus

Regular blender, immersion blender, or food processor

How You Make It:

1. First, place all the ingredients in your instant pot and stir to combine.

2. Next, close the lid, select slow cook and set the LOW. Cook for 6 to 7 hours.

3. When done, puree with the help of an immersion blender or transferring the ketchup to a blender or food processor.

4. After that, transfer to resealable jars and allow to cool completely, then seal and refrigerate.

Chicken Tikka Masala

Serves 4 to 6

Ingredients:

1 to 1 ½ pounds boneless, skinless chicken thighs (cut into bite-size pieces)

1 large onion (diced)

1-inch piece whole ginger (peeled & grated)

3 cloves garlic (minced)

1 to 2 tbsp garam masala

1 (28-oz.) can diced tomatoes

2 tbsp tomato paste

2 tsp paprika

2 tsp kosher salt

¾ cup heavy cream or coconut milk

Fresh cilantro (chopped)

2 cups cooked rice, to serve

How You Make It:

1. Simply, add the chicken, onion, garlic, ginger, 1 tbsp of garam masala, tomato paste, paprika, and salt and stir until the chicken is evenly covered with spices.

2. Add the diced tomatoes with their juices.

3. Ideally, you can choose the marinate the chicken in ½ cup yogurt for 6 to 8 hours. After which you shake to remove excess yogurt before adding to cooker.

4. Also, you might want to first, sauté the onions and garlic before using in a little olive oil using the saute function or in a skillet. Then, stir in the ginger, tomato

paste, and spices until fragrant. After which you can then transfer to the instant pot.

5. Cover and cook for 4 hours on high or 8 hours on low. Then, 15 mins before the end of cooking, you open and stir in the heavy cream.

6. Could be served over rice with fresh cilantro sprinkled over.

Chicken Minestrone

Ingredients

2 large bone-in chicken breast

2 garlic cloves (crushed)

2 boxes chicken broth (32 oz. each)

1 onion (diced)

1 can diced tomatoes

2-3 carrots (sliced)

2 cups kale (chopped)

1 can dark, red kidney beans

1 zucchini (chopped)

¾ cup shell pasta

salt and pepper to taste

Parmesan cheese for topping (optional)

How You Make It:

1. Simply place the chicken breasts, onion, garlic, tomatoes, chicken broth and carrot in your IP duo plus.

2. Select slow cook and cook on high 5-6 hours or low 7-8 hours.

3. When done, mins before serving, remove the chicken breasts and add zucchini, pasta and kale to cooker.

4. Separate the chicken from bone using a fork and shred the meat.

5. Return to cooker when done and season with salt and pepper.

6. Divide into bowls and top each bowl with Parmesan if using.

French Onion Soup

Serves: 6

Ingredients

3 pounds yellow onions (peeled, sliced, & cut into quarter-moons)

2 tbsp olive oil

1 tsp salt (+more to taste)

2 tbsp balsamic vinegar

2 tbsp unsalted butter (melted)

Freshly ground black pepper

10 cups beef broth

3 tbsp brandy (optional)

To Serve

4 to 6 baguette slices (toasted, for each bowl)

1 1/3 to 2 cups grated Gruyere cheese (1/3 cup per bowl)

Chopped shallot or fresh onion

How You Make It:

1. Add onion, butter, olive oil, salt, and black pepper to your instant pot and cover.

2. Select slow cook and cook on LOW for 12 hours.

3. After that, stir in the broth and balsamic vinegar.

4. Cover and cook for 6 to 8 hours on LOW.

5. Season with more salt and pepper if needed and stir in the brandy if using.

6. Now, heat the to 350°F. Transfer soup into oven-safe bowls and place them in a baking pan.

7. Top each bowl with a slice of the toast and shredded Gruyere cheese.

8. Bake this for 20 to 30 mins on a rack in the upper third of your oven until the cheese is completely melted.

9. Once that is achieved, turn the oven to broil and broil until the cheese is bubbling and browned (2 to 3 mins).

10. Remove and allow to cool for a few mins before serving with chopped fresh onion on the side.

CHAPTER 12: DESSERT & CAKES

Chocolate Mousse Cheesecake

Prep time: 15 m

Cook time: 1 h

Ready In: 1 d 1 h 15 m

10 servings

454 cals

Ingredients

½ cup chocolate cookie crumbs

8 (1 oz.) squares semisweet chocolate

2 (8 oz.) packages cream cheese (softened)

1 pinch ground cinnamon

1 tbsp butter

1 tsp vanilla extract

2 eggs, beaten

1 cup heavy whipping cream

2/3 cup white sugar

1 ½ tbsp unsweetened cocoa powder

1 ½ cups water

How You Make It:

1. First, grease an 8-inch springform pan that fits inside your instant pot.

2. Next, you mix together the chocolate wafer crumbs and cinnamon. Sprinkle this on the bottom of the springform pan and press gently to form the crust.

3. When done, melt the chocolate and butter together and set aside.

4. Now, using a food processor, process cream cheese until smooth and add the chocolate mixture from step 3.

5. Process until the mixture becomes uniformly colored.

6. Proceed by pouring in the cream, sugar, vanilla extract and eggs. Beat well and sieve the cocoa powder over batter.

7. After that, pulse on low speed until cocoa blends in. Pour mixture over crumbs in pan.

8. At this point, cover cake with a piece of waxed paper and wrap the pan completely with aluminum foil.

9. Prepare your instant pot and add water it. Insert the trivet and place pan on it

10. Secure the lid and pressure cook at high for 50 mins (Use natural release).

11. Take out the cheesecake and let cool to room temperature.

12. Remove from pan and refrigerate for 8 hours before serving.

Brownie Cake

Prep time: 10 mins
Cook time: 18 mins
Total time: 28 mins
Serves: 4

Ingredients

4 tbsp unsalted butter

⅔ Cup Sugar (for sugar-free, use erythritol)

¼ tsp vanilla extract

2 tbsp chocolate chips (for sugar-free, use stevia-sweetened chips)

2 Eggs

½ cup all-purpose flour (for gluten-free, use Bob's Red Mill 1-1 baking blend)

4 tbsp cocoa powder (for sugar-free, use unsweetened cocoa powder)

2 tbsp powdered sugar (optional)

How You Make It:

1. First, microwave the butter and chocolate chips in microwave-safe bowl for 1 minute until melted.

2. After that, beat butter, chocolate chips and sugar in a bowl until well combined. Add egg, vanilla and continue until blended.

3. Next, Sift Flour, cocoa over them and mix.

4. Place a rack in your instant pot, add 1-cup of water to it and transfer the batter to ramekins after which you place them on the rack.

5.   Cover the tops of with foil and seal the cooker lid.

6. Cook at high pressure for 18 mins + quick release.

7. Top with powdered sugar

Duo Plus Applesauce

Prep: 25 mins | Cook: 5 mins | Total: 30 mins

Ingredients

3 pounds Organic Gala Apple (quartered, peeled or unpeeled)

1 – 2 cinnamon stick(s)

¼ cup water

¼ - ½ tsp (0.5 g - 1 g) nutmeg

A pinch of salt

Honey to taste

How You Make It:

1. First, place cinnamon stick(s), nutmeg, water and apples into your instant pot and close the lid.

2. Cook at High Pressure for 5 mins + Natural Release.

3. Open the lid and remove cinnamon stick(s). Blend the applesauce with an immersion blender.

4. Add a pinch of salt and honey to taste.

Duo Plus Chocolate Peanut Butter Cake

Ingredients

1 Chocolate Cake Mix (We used Devil's Food or German Chocolate)

1 (10-12oz.) can 100% Pure Pumpkin

½ cup Peanut Butter

1 cup Water

Ingredients for Icing:

1 8 oz. container Whipped Topping

⅛ cup Peanut Butter

1 package chocolate pudding

How You Make It:

1. First, spray an 8-inch springform pan with non-stick cooking spray and set aside.

2. Combine cake mix, pumpkin, peanut butter, and water in a bowl. Pour into pan from step 1.

3. Add 1 cup water to your Duo plus Instant Pot and make a sling for lowering the pan into your instant pot (Can be done by folding an aluminon foil lengthwise).

4. Place pan into the Instant Pot using the sling to make for easy removal.

5. Secure the lid and cook at High pressure for 30 mins (use 15 mins natural + quick release).

6. Open the lid and remove pan. Allow to cool completely before icing.

For Icing;

1. Mix dry chocolate pudding mix with peanut butter in a bowl.

2. After mixing, slowly fold into the whipped topping. And then, pipe icing onto the top of cake, using a piping bag and tip of choice.

MEASUREMENT CONVERSIONS & ABBREVIATIONS

Abbreviations

oz = oz

fl oz = fluid oz

tsp =tsp

tbsp = tbsp

ml = milliliter

c = cup

pt = pint

qt = quart

gal = gallon

L = liter

PC = Pressure Cooker

ePC = Electric Pressure Cooker

QPR = Quick Pressure Release

NPR = Natural Pressure Release

Conversions

1/2 fl oz = 3 tsp = 1 tbsp = 15 ml

1 fl oz = 2 tbsp = 1/ 8 c = 30 ml

2 fl oz = 4 tbsp = 1/ 4 c = 60 ml

4 fl oz = 8 tbsp = 1/ 2 c = 118 ml

8 fl oz = 16 tbsp = 1 c = 236 ml

16 fl oz = 1 pt = 1/ 2 qt = 2 c = 473 ml

128 fl oz = 8 pt = 4 qt = 1 gal = 3.78 L

THE END

.